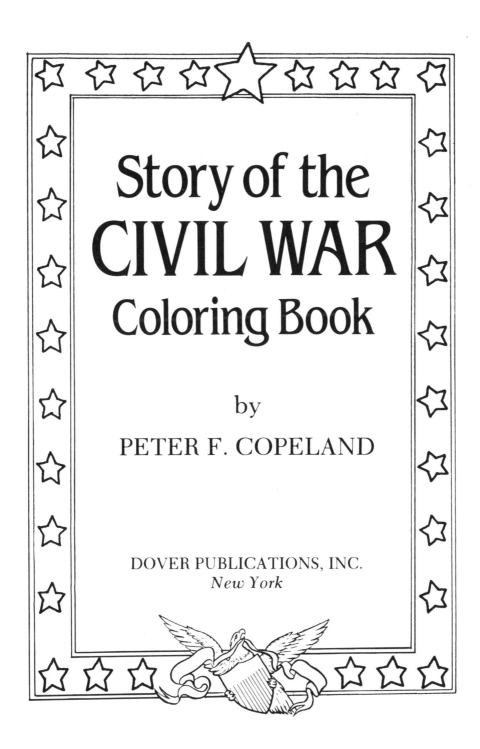

Story of the CIVIL WAR Coloring Book

by

PETER F. COPELAND

DOVER PUBLICATIONS, INC.
New York

TO BRYAN PAUL JADOT,
whose ancestor was Captain Eliazer Taylor,
Co. H ("The Marion Volunteers"),
46th Georgia Volunteer Infantry Regiment, C.S.A.

Published in Canada by General Publishing Company, Ltd., 30 Lesmill Road, Don Mills, Toronto, Ontario.

Story of the Civil War Coloring Book is a new work, first published by Dover Publications, Inc., in 1991.

DOVER *Pictorial Archive* SERIES

This book belongs to the Dover Pictorial Archive Series. You may use the designs and illustrations for graphics and crafts applications, free and without special permission, provided that you include no more than four in the same publication or project. (For permission for additional use, please write to Dover Publications, Inc., 31 East 2nd Street, Mineola, N.Y. 11501.)

However, republication or reproduction of any illustration by any other graphic service whether it be in a book or in any other design resource is strictly prohibited.

International Standard Book Number: 0-486-26532-3

Manufactured in the United States of America
Dover Publications, Inc., 31 East 2nd Street, Mineola, N.Y. 11501

INTRODUCTION

THE AMERICAN CIVIL WAR, known in the North also as the War of the Rebellion and in the South as the War Between the States, was fought, in the main, over the issue of slavery.

Slavery became a cause of contention in the U.S. as early as 1820, with America's expansion into the West. The Missouri Compromise preserved the balance of slave and free states entering the Union from the new territories of the West, but the slavery issue became steadily more and more explosive. Texas entered the Union as a slave state in 1845 and the Compromise of 1850 divided the territories won in the Mexican War.

Antislavery sentiment grew steadily hotter, fed by such incidents as the publication of Harriet Beecher Stowe's abolitionist novel *Uncle Tom's Cabin* in 1852; the Dred Scott Decision of 1857; and the undeclared war that raged in Kansas between slave- and free-state forces.

Soon after the election of the Republican candidate Abraham Lincoln to the presidency in 1860, South Carolina seceded from the United States, on December 20. Mississippi, Florida, Alabama, Georgia, Louisiana and Texas followed South Carolina, and regional militia forces in these seceding states seized United States forts, weapons and ammunition depots. On April 15, 1861, President Lincoln called upon the loyal states to furnish 75,000 volunteer soldiers to end the rebellion of the seceding Southern states. This was seen by the South as a declaration of war. Tennessee, North Carolina, Arkansas and Virginia joined their sister Southern states in secession, bringing the rebellious states to eleven in number.

The first shot of the war was fired by the Southern forces at Fort Sumter in Charleston harbor in 1861, and the last shots were fired in 1865, in Texas, near Palo Alto, between Confederate troops and the 63rd U.S. Regiment of Colored Troops. The last man wounded in the war was Sergeant Crocker, a black soldier.

During the American Civil War, the loss on both sides of able-bodied men killed outright, mortally wounded, dead of disease or wounded to incapacity was over one million.

The total cost of the four-year conflict has been estimated as over eight billion dollars in modern currency. It was, and remains to the present day, America's bloodiest war.

A slave auction of 1860. One of the most tragic aspects of slavery was the slave auction, where members of families were often forcibly separated and sold to buyers hundreds of miles apart, never to see one another again. A healthy young field hand might bring as much as a thousand dollars at such an auction.

Harriet Tubman and Frederick Douglass. Harriet Tubman (ca. 1821–1913) escaped from slavery in 1849. She was an organizer of the Underground Railroad, assisting slaves to escape bondage by hiding them and transporting them into the Northern states and Canada. Frederick Douglass (1817–1895), also an escaped slave, founded a weekly newspaper in the North and campaigned throughout his life for the abolition of slavery.

The storming of Harpers Ferry. A band of abolitionists led by John Brown took over the U.S. Army arsenal at Harpers Ferry, Virginia (now West Virginia), in October 1859, with the intention of beginning and arming a slave uprising that they hoped would spread like wildfire throughout the South. The abolitionists were driven from the arsenal and arrested by a unit of U.S. Marines led by Colonel Robert E. Lee of the U.S. Army.

The 1860 election of Abraham Lincoln. The election to the presidency of Abraham Lincoln (1809–1865), favored candidate of the antislavery faction in the North, inflamed Southerners. On December 20, 1860, South Carolina seceded from the Union.

The Confederate White House at Montgomery, Alabama. The rebellious Southern states that followed South Carolina out of the Union set up an independent government, the Confederate States of America, with Jefferson Davis (1808–1889) as president. Here the Confederate president and his cabinet greet the crowd in the new capital of Montgomery, Alabama (Montgomery remained the Confederate capital for less than four months).

The bombardment of Fort Sumter. Confederate forces in South Carolina demanded the surrender of the U.S. Army garrison at Fort Sumter in Charleston harbor on April 12, 1861. When the commander, Major Robert Anderson, refused to comply with their demands, the Southerners opened artillery fire upon the island fort. With his food supplies exhausted and Fort Sumter in flames, Anderson finally surrendered on April 13. The bombardment of Fort Sumter signaled the beginning of the Civil War.

9

The 6th Massachusetts Regiment attacked by a mob in Baltimore. On April 19, 1861, a mob of Southern sympathizers attacked the 6th Massachusetts Regiment in the streets of Baltimore as that regiment was en route to Washington, D.C. In the battle that followed, twenty of the rioters and four soldiers were killed.

Recruiting volunteers for the army. Recruiting stations opened in major cities and towns north and south. There was no shortage of volunteers to enlist in that first year of the war. As the years passed, as battles were fought and casualties mounted, the flow of volunteers nearly ceased, and both sides were forced to enact conscription laws, drafting men to replace casualties and to form new regiments.

11

The First Battle of Bull Run. On July 20, 1861, the first great battle of the Civil War was fought near Manassas in northern Virginia. The Southern army won a decisive victory, and the roads to Washington were clogged with fleeing soldiers and with civilians who had come out from the capital to see the fight.

The *Trent* affair. On November 8, 1861, Captain Charles Wilkes of the U.S. Navy, aboard the *San Jacinto*, boarded the British mail steamer *Trent* and removed two Confederate commissioners, James Mason and John Slidell, who were on their way to Europe to seek support for the Southern cause. War with England threatened until Secretary of State William H. Seward ordered the captured Confederates released.

Grant takes Fort Donelson. Union forces in the West aimed at opening the Mississippi River, thus splitting the Confederacy in half. Brigadier General Ulysses S. Grant, in a brilliant campaign, captured Fort Henry on the Tennessee River and Fort Donelson on the Cumberland in February 1862. At Fort Donelson Grant sent the encircled Southern commander this message: "No terms except unconditional and immediate surrender can be accepted. I propose to move immediately upon your works."

The *Monitor* and the *Merrimac*. The United States frigate *Merrimac*, lying at the Norfolk, Virginia, Navy Yard, was captured by the Confederates and converted into an ironclad warship (renamed the *Virginia*). On March 8, 1862, the rebel ironclad attacked the wooden U.S. Navy ships at Hampton Roads, Virginia, and might have destroyed them all but for the arrival on the scene of the United States Navy ironclad *Monitor*. The two ironclad warships fought an epic battle that ended in a draw. Two months later the *Merrimac* was destroyed by her Confederate crew to prevent her capture by U.S. Navy forces at Newport News, Virginia.

The Battle of Shiloh. In April 1862 a surprise Confederate attack upon the army of General Grant at Shiloh on the Tennessee River caught the Union troops unprepared and a furious battle developed. Grant managed to rally his men, call up reinforcements and turn the tide of battle in favor of the North, after the Confederate commander, General Albert Sidney Johnston, was mortally wounded.

The Battle of Malvern Hill. Meanwhile, in Virginia, Union forces advancing upon Richmond, the new Confederate capital, came so close that they could hear the alarm bells ringing within the city. In a brilliant series of battles, the Southern army, led by Generals Joseph E. Johnston and Robert E. Lee, managed to drive back the Union army in the so-called Seven Days' Campaign. At Malvern Hill (on July 1, 1862), the last of these battles, the Union army won a victory, but did not follow it up, and retreated to its base at Harrison's Landing.

Recruiting former slaves for the Union army. Liberated and runaway slaves were enlisted in the Union armies as early as 1862 in occupied areas of Louisiana and South Carolina. With the signing of the Emancipation Proclamation in January 1863, recruiting of black soldiers got under way on a large scale. By the end of that year fifty black regiments were already in existence. Two hundred thousand black soldiers served in the Union armies before the end of the war.

The Second Battle of Bull Run. In August 1862, the Army of Northern Virginia, led by General Robert E. Lee, attacked General John Pope's Union Army of Virginia on the old battlefield of Bull Run in Virginia, called by the Southerners Manassas, and won another brilliant victory. Once again the Union army retreated to Washington.

The Battle of Antietam. General Lee led the Army of Northern Virginia across the Potomac River into Maryland in an invasion of the North in September 1862. At Sharpsburg, Maryland, a terrible two-day battle was fought on the 17th and 18th of September near Antietam Creek, the bloodiest battle of the war so far. On the evening of September 18, Lee retreated back across the Potomac into Virginia, leaving the Union army in possession of the battlefield.

The Ambulance Corps of the Army of the Potomac. Soon after the bloody battle of Antietam, Federal authorities organized and equipped the Ambulance Corps to assist the Medical Department in transporting and caring for the wounded. Here we see an ambulance drill of the new and well-equipped Corps.

The Emancipation Proclamation. Signed in a preliminary version by President Lincoln in September 1862, the Emancipation Proclamation declared all slaves residing within the territory of the Confederacy legally free persons as of January 1, 1863. Slavery continued legal, however, in those loyal states where it had already existed and in those areas of the Confederacy occupied by the Union army, as long as the war lasted.

THE INFANTRY

USA CSA

The infantry. The infantryman bore the heaviest burden of combat and mortality. His weapon was generally a muzzle-loading single-shot musket and bayonet. He lived mainly on hardtack and coffee (when he could get it). Any other food he received was issued raw, and the soldier cooked it himself in his tin cup. Fresh meat and vegetables were issued only rarely. The infantryman marched to war loaded down with a canteen and tin cup; a knapsack or blanket roll; cartridge box and forty rounds of ammunition; a bayonet; a haversack; a cap box; and (if he was lucky) a rubber poncho. A wound often meant death or amputation. The infantry soldier often went to war a green recruit, but he learned fast if he survived, and he fought in the greatest battles ever seen on American soil.

The Battle of Chancellorsville. After the defeat of the Union Army of the Potomac at Fredericksburg in December 1862, General Joseph Hooker assumed command. At Chancellorsville in May 1863, Robert E. Lee, with a Southern army half the size of Hooker's Army of the Potomac, outwitted the Union commander and won a battle that should have been a Northern victory. The South paid a heavy price for the victory, however, with the death of General Thomas J. "Stonewall" Jackson, seen here advancing with his men on the flank of the Federal Eleventh Corps.

The Union naval blockade. President Lincoln proclaimed a naval blockade of the Southern coastline from Virginia to Texas two weeks after the fall of Fort Sumter in 1861. By mid-1862 the blockade of Confederate seaports began to become really effective, capturing and destroying the fast blockade-running ships seeking to bring desperately needed supplies into Southern ports. Ports along the Southern coastline were bombarded by the Federal fleet and largely reduced to ruins.

The New York City draft riots. The city of New York was wracked by four days of uncontrollable mob violence in July of 1863. The mobs, protesting inequities in the military draft and inflamed by Southern sympathizers called Copperheads, looted ships, burned down buildings, including a black orphanage, and attacked and murdered African-Americans in the streets. Federal troops had to be called in to restore order.

The Battle of Gettysburg. Robert E. Lee invaded Pennsylvania in June of 1863, hoping, by threatening Washington and Philadelphia, to break Northern morale and finally to gain recognition and independence for the Southern Confederacy. At Gettysburg, Pennsylvania, Lee's Army of Northern Virginia met the Army of the Potomac, now under General George G. Meade, in the most famous battle ever fought on American soil. After three days of heavy fighting, the Southerners were turned back and again retreated into Virginia.

The Siege of Vicksburg. In the West, General Grant spent the last months of 1862 and much of the first half of 1863 trying to capture the Confederate stronghold of Vicksburg on the Mississippi River. Finally, on July 4, 1863, after a brilliant three-month campaign, Vicksburg fell. Here we see fugitives under the fire of Union artillery during the final six-week-long siege and bombardment. With the defeat at Gettysburg in the East and the fall of Vicksburg in the West, Southern hopes were beginning to die.

The Battle of Chickamauga. In September 1863 the Union Army of the Cumberland at Chickamauga Creek in Tennessee might have been completely destroyed by the Confederate army under General Braxton Bragg but for the steadiness and bravery of troops under the command of General George Thomas, seen here observing the battle from the Union artillery lines. Thomas was forever afterward remembered as the "Rock of Chickamauga." 31

The cavalry. The horse soldiers were the scouts, the eyes of the armies. They were also raiders, capturing and destroying war material and supplies in the rear areas. At the beginning of the war the Confederate cavalry was the superior mounted force, but, as the war progressed, the Northern cavalry eventually matched and overcame the best the South could put in the field. Muzzle-loading and breech-loading carbines, six-shooter revolvers and sabers were the favorite weapons of the horse soldiers, though some Southern mounted men were partial to shotguns. The cavalry participated in battle, fighting sometimes dismounted, as infantry.

Grant appointed Commander-in-Chief of all Union armies. In March 1864 President Lincoln appointed General Ulysses S. Grant commander of all the Union armies. Grant then appointed General William T. Sherman to command the Western armies, while General George G. Meade remained in command of the armies of the East.

The Battle of the Wilderness. Once more, in the spring of 1864, the Army of the Potomac advanced upon Richmond. In a month of fighting in the Wilderness region of Virginia, the Union gained little and lost much in casualties. Here we see Union artillerymen repelling a Confederate night attack.

The Battle of Cold Harbor. Hoping to turn the flank of the Army of Northern Virginia in his advance upon Richmond, Grant assaulted the Southern army at Cold Harbor on June 3, 1864. The attack was called off after the Union army suffered terrible casualties crossing open ground under heavy Southern fire.

Lincoln reelected president. The presidential campaign of 1864 saw Abraham Lincoln elected for a second term as president of the United States. Here the president takes his oath of office for his second term, administered by Chief Justice Salmon P. Chase.

The Battle of Atlanta. During the summer of 1864 General Sherman fought a series of battles before the city of Atlanta, driving back the defending Confederate army and beginning a forty-day siege of the city. Atlanta fell to Sherman on September 2, and on November 15 Sherman burned much of the city before leaving to begin his march to the sea. Here we see Confederate troops in their fortified lines on the city's outskirts.

Sherman's march through Georgia to the sea. During the march through Georgia that followed the fall of Atlanta, Sherman's army lived off the land, raiding, looting and destroying farms, crops and plantations, leaving in its wake a path of ruin and destruction. Sherman reached Savannah and the sea in December 1864.

THE NAVY

The navy. In addition to enforcing the Federal blockade of Southern seacoasts, the Union navy fought its war on the deep sea, pursuing Confederate maritime raiders, and in coastal waters, along rivers and inland waterways, cooperating with the operations of the army. Before the war was over, the U.S. Navy had dozens of ironclad warships like the *Monitor* patrolling the rivers and coastlines as part of the blockading fleet.

Here we see a Confederate naval officer (top left), a U.S. Navy "powder monkey" (center; a young boy who helped serve the guns) and a U.S. marine in dress uniform. Also shown are a naval cutlass (right), a boarding axe, a Federal gunboat of the blockading fleet (top right) and a steam-driven wooden sailing sloop of war.

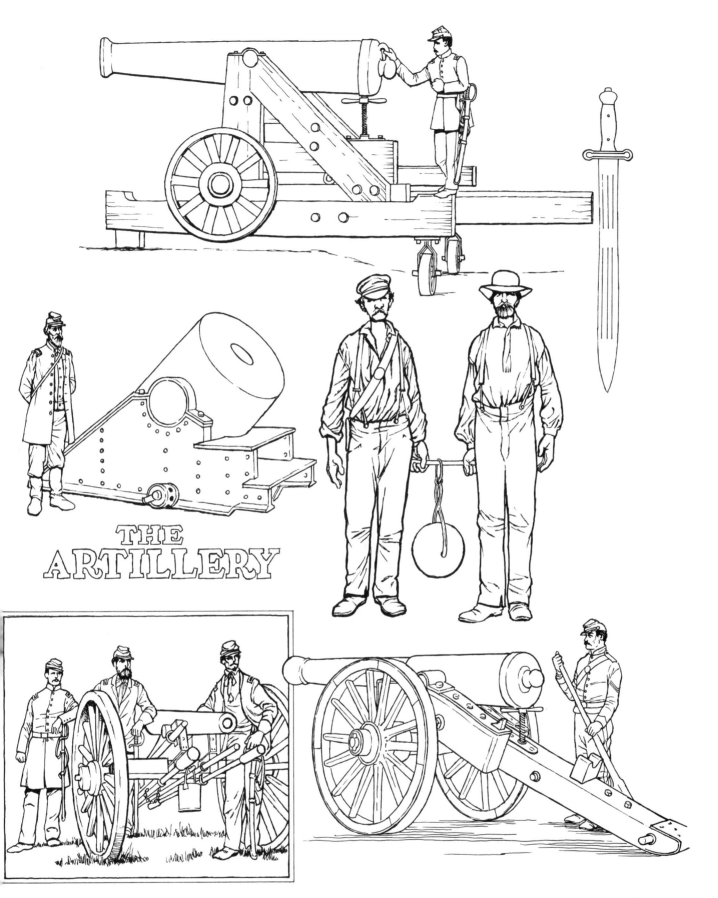

The artillery. The model 1857 smoothbore Napoleon howitzer was the most mobile and versatile fieldpiece used by both sides during the war, but both North and South also used rifled artillery pieces of great accuracy, massive siege and garrison guns and mortars of many different sizes. At the top of the page we see a large fortress gun mounted on a wooden barbette carriage. Center left is a thirteen-inch seacoast mortar. At the bottom is a twelve-pound bronze Napoleon howitzer (left) and a twenty-four-pound gun on a siege carriage.

41

A Rebel sea raider. Southern commerce raiders attacked U.S. vessels wherever they found them. A number of warships like the C.S.S. *Alabama,* seen here, were built in English shipyards for the Confederate government. Here we see the *Alabama* after having burned a U.S. merchant ship in the North Atlantic.

The Siege of Petersburg. Unable to break through the defense lines before Richmond, General Grant and General Meade's Army of the Potomac moved around to the south of the Confederate capital and laid siege to the town of Petersburg in June of 1864. The winter of 1864–65 saw the Union army still in the siege lines; despite numerous attacks like the one seen here, they could not break through. Petersburg held out for over nine months before General Lee was forced to retreat toward Lynchburg, abandoning Petersburg, as well as Richmond, to the Union forces on the night of April 2–3, 1865.

Lee surrenders at Appomattox. Lee now realized that the war was lost. He surrendered the outnumbered Army of Northern Virginia to Grant, signing the articles of capitulation at Appomattox Court House, Virginia, on April 9, 1865. Before the end of May all remaining Confederate forces in the field surrendered and the Civil War was over.

The assassination of President Lincoln. On the evening of Good Friday, April 14, 1865, President Abraham Lincoln was assassinated while attending a performance at Ford's Theatre in Washington, D.C. The assassin was a talented but mentally unbalanced actor and Southern sympathizer named John Wilkes Booth. Pursued by Union soldiers twelve days later, Booth, escaping from a burning barn, was fatally shot by one of them (some say he shot himself).

Grand review of the armies, Washington, D.C. On May 23–24, 1865, the Union armies of the East and West marched in a grand review, celebrating their victory, down Pennsylvania Avenue in Washington, D.C. It was the most magnificent parade the capital had ever seen, and it marked the end of America's bloodiest war.